T0199003

To order additional copies of this book, contact:
Xlibris
1-888-795-4274
www.Xlibris.com
Orders@Xlibris.com

ISBN: 978-1-9845-8546-2 (sc)
ISBN: 978-1-9845-8545-5 (e)

Print information available on the last page

Rev. date: 07/09/2020

She DID Rise

BY

SHANNON GOWENS

In Love is not a choice

We love many in our time - pieces, parts, reflections of what we admire, strive towards, and learn from
Love has some reason - some control. Some rational understanding
In love is raw - without choice or reasonable logic
Falling in love is lovely, painful, terrifying, frustrating, and completely irrational and so beautiful
My in love has no reasoning - no rules
It's wild abandonment to something so rare and unbridled
In love is not a choice - it's the part of us we don't understand or can control
It's shameless and can not play hard to get
It's vulnerable and when viewed from outside seems uncharacteristic by our friends. Ridiculous. Compromising
and settling sometimes
But true in love drives to love. To sit with love. Simply for a kiss. Even risks rejection. Embarrassment. Because it
can not un know the feeling. Beyond rational and reason
To wait for a lover who wants space. To stay distant from any emotional attempts.
Swooning lovers and suitors. Deep affection and commitment. Such attention and obsession - only to be reminded
that her desire is bound, heartbroken, and chained like a willing slave to another soul. No amount of devotion can
severe the connection
It's strange to watch others fall over themselves for any sign - time, text, even a smile - when the sought after lover
can't open up or see them this way - she wants to. She understands this is respect, affection, and true appreciation.
Valuable. But she can't. She is foolish in love - like a young girl on a beach watching the sea - she waits always.
Even for love she has - she waits because she can't not. Her cells hold her there - and she tries to reason - to run
because she is smart and capable of anything
But she can't un know in love
So she doesn't hide - she opens and let's 'in love' have her unconditionally
Fearfully
Vulnerably
Because she knows no other way

The path is rocky

The path is rocky. The path is rough
Sweeping the pebbles. Though never enough
gravel - rock - stone. Jagged and coarse,
Trudging through daggers, Sheerly by force

Where do I run?
Where do I go?

Dig, dig, dig...digging the hole
Ripping off polish. Clawing at gold
Dig, dig, dig...digging the hole
Tearing up comfort. Reckless unfold
Dig, dig, dig...digging the hole
Where is the bottom? Turn round and hope holds
First handful of sand to rebuild my soul

Tragic

Obsession, desire - is a limited fire
Smoldering bright - once acquired- retired
Imagination it seems is not that of dreams
Earthly ground and grit, not moonlighted beams
The comedy here - we all know each side
Chasing the dream or running to hide
Often one side is familiar for some
While the scales lay unbalanced - not yet undone
I know well the mountains - long lingered a top
Dismissive and careless of hearts I might stop
Most climb and move on but that day one did not
A shadow - first unnoticed, then puzzling thoughts
A decade of standing became a soft touch
Then kisses and wooing - deep affections and trust
But his long standing grew weary as she leaned on his skin
He decided to sit - a few paces within
Down the slope but not off it - just enough to be seen
So she left her ground long held to chase the old love dream
She walked not far to reach him - but then he walked a bit more
She did this so often he seemed now to ignore
The devotion, affection, selfless acts still from her
It seemed long desire and love now a blur
So here's the piece - the thing - my gift, learn from me
If you are on a mountain, don't chase men to the sea

My Heart (Fire)

Strength and spark
Bright spark! Fireworks in the dark
Commanding - ironic
Brightness - being bright - looks out
Only sees dull, dingy, grey
This is the world - but this is not who she is
She is choreographed chaos
A symphony - raw, unique, primal
Pulsating - organic - clawing to acquire
Something she already is
Bursting light - impulsive beacon
Meant to burn blindly - boldly
Hold that flame dear love
Fear drives you to embellish and seek out cheap attention - known attention - common attention
Hear me
You are not common - trust your expression, passion, and fearless fire
Contained and commanded - without self doubt
Quiet confidence the world has never known - surely needs - and no one could ignore
I see the spark - always have - don't tame your flames

My Heart (Earth)

Ease, such ease - smooth like soft rock
Rolled through a river - without struggle or statement
No sharp edges - just soft footprints
Tender petals naturally plucked by a soft breeze
Delicate and quiet ground
The illusion of weakness- comforts and gentle song birds
But deep, dormant Phoenix - unknown to even the vessel
Greatest strength - stones collect to make mountains
Slow - steady - remarkable
Unstoppable force - once realized course
Self doubt- shame - shadows
Diluted - muddied - clouds
All false! True self here reflects foundation
Unfaltering - unwavering
Humble servant
Fear of untapped potential
Fear not - pebbles and sand quietly sculpt landscapes - brushing seashore with soft memories
And hillside with nearly depthless dreams
Such warm, complex dreams
My greatest comfort is to revel in them
Her dreams - only hers
Pull them to my chin - like a childhood blanket
And let go - pure trust. Let go - for a sacred and simple cuddle

My heart (Air)

I can not express in words sometimes
The secrets of my heart
Those who touch it
Submerse in it
Hold large segments - they are few
I have recently learned
My feelings are delicate - subtle
I yearn to run from them - and all grounding
Inhaling passion - pulling, mindless current
Travel - surrender - suspend
But all light spirits eventually exhale - creating presence and brief weight
Toes grazing dusty soil lead way to heel strike, heavy mind - facing mindful moment
I find myself screaming - the world hears a whisper -
I wish they heard nothing
My deepest, dearest loves often go unnoticed
Unfelt -
But they move me, touch me, and break me without intention.
I wish to uproot- to avoid genuine emotions
Because I do scream and I do feel - quietly but deeply
So much so when they hurt my eyes water
And when they bleed my heart breaks

IXIES explores a whole new world—a of magic charged with the wild of creatures who do not live by rules. Theirs is a realm of delight, and ench...

...fted artists who ...Lee and Brian Fr... of the history o... ...ources, they exa... ...ds, sorted fact ... ...minated their fi... ...undred extraor... ...olor paintings. ...tistry combin... ...result.

...identified and ...elves, pixies, ...dryads, and ...on their favori... ...of life are ...m the great ...nguage, ...ong these ...s the ...Yeats's ...and

Seduction

Fingertips on skin caress collarbone
Pale, light as thread. Trailing subtle touch
Lingering goosebumps - raised, reaching
Air through parted teeth like fogging a mirror
Chin tilting without conscious effort
Light lips whisper kisses - neck, earlobe, soft cheek - hinting, asking.
A turn by magnetic force to fold into embrace and connection

My wrists

I offer them up
Together turned - vulnerable
Slow - eye lids follow

Steady love

Some love builds - like layers
Delicate, complex, unique
Grandiose gestures - perhaps rarely
More often subtle, simple, with meaning unnoticed
Often unappreciated
So hear me - those lovers of duration, endurance
Willing compromise
Love - beautiful love
You are the bearer - the fruit - ripe definition
And devotion
Where cells reach out to connect
Where one exhale matches their inhale
As ocean meets sand
Fingertips search true loves hand

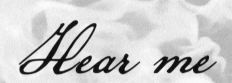

Hear me

Hear my voice without words
Shoulders raised - no enter
Tightened muscles form walls
Blocking, bracing - touch stalled
Persistence tightens - tense
One sided lust - sensed
Not asking her needs
Deep longing - never freed

Don't ask - don't wonder

Every milestone and wrinkle
They mark and raise time
Bring forth prominent meaning
Observation
Contemplation
But don't wonder - don't ask
Don't burden yourself
Heavy thoughts and slow memories
Hold them gently - no guilt
No questions or puzzles
Live lightly and loving
Hold me - with sweet stories
And ask nothing of why
Because some souls have purpose
And destiny knows no blame

Anger

Shortened breath, first
Undefined complexity and intentions
Burrowing - deep, sought out emotions
Send quick snarl and curled fists
Fingernails digging into palms - sharp
Leaving pale hands and red marks
Teeth - awaiting something - perhaps primal
A guttural growl escapes on low notes
Tense, prepping, searching
Where to direct - this release
The walls take the burden now
Searching release - mild satisfaction
Unburdening requires direction, intention and true source - burning aim

Showing up

I love you. Just as you are
I sense uncertainty - like guilt for something self judged
Beaten enough to doubt- and to silently ask
For validation, friendship and love
They're not sure they deserve it
Shadows of nervous patterns
Because bottoms drop out
And have
But the worst is behind you
Heal - and gain grounding
Know the planet is better because of you
I am better because of you
I never fear you - you embrace my heart

First lost

The first time you lose a close love - Irreplaceable presence
A piece of your planet
Earth splinters and shifts
Repositions and forces new patterns
New life - delicate adjustments
And you eventually realize
That there will be no more new memories
No more photos
No more videos
Just nostalgic evenings with those who barely remember
Watching - patching the fragments
Scratch to remember walking blurry gardens and the breeze of a park merry go round
A swing so high - invoking fear and determination to overcome it without knowing why - brief moment of flight
Long phone calls - monologues
And eccentric affection
Unique, complicated intentions
Unsettled in himself, so unable to organize or focus
But wrapped in unavailable, misdirected, and misplaced anger
Ill prepared and inappropriate marks
Lay small growth
Unforeseen seed
Quiet repentance and love
Mutual love
Love that bonded, connected, softened
And one day forgave
Gratitude remained
And years of obsession - lesson learned of loss
Love despite anger, mistreatment, dismissal, and all unfair events
Because at the end, love brings peace

I wish

You could feel the layers of my heart
The shameless obsession I have
With you
I'm here
I'm not going anywhere
Hold me - hold my complex emotions
Kiss me - place your hands around my face
And acknowledge - recognize my blind love for you
And then sharply awaken - remember
Each breathe - each mindful moment
Every cell on my skin
I offer -slowly
And I desire you
Even when I pretend I don't
Say words that imply stoic cold expression
But eventually I can't pretend
I have something to offer - privately
I want only you to know
I'm yours - completely and blindly

Dragon

Spring morning in childhood
Glancing out window without cause or care
Right corner - fleeting maturity of petals
Full, and crinkled
Royal - deep purple
So many iris varieties are sleek
Thin, tight like shearing scissor blades
Disciplined and unforgiving -
Cold - but fair. Direct and balanced -
But this right corner
From my window
My childhood garden
This iris is scandalous
Unnecessarily feathered and pouting
Plump - incandescent
Deliciously stretched
This is my favorite - my iris
This iris is called dragon

I am my own

I am my own and I am strong.
I need no one or ask anyone to do anything for me
But I love you - unconditionally, inexplicably, without rhyme or reason
I can't change it or stop it
Because true love has no logical space
So I argue because it gives me a sense of boundaries
I get quiet or polite so I have the illusion of self control

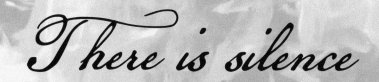

There is silence

When music stops and lights dim out
Base wilters and sparkle dulls
The quiet before redudance
Repeat agitation for nightlife vibration
Humming like bees in a barrel
Anticipating a release - fruition
But that is later - now is silence

Stone is soft

They don't see it - the true image
A turning of earth, light, and attention
Unwanted
Unasked for
Commanding - natural strength and dismissal
Bubbling and layered
Nothing cheap or patched together
A deep brewing of person
A scratched layer leaves remaining strong levels
Rings - tightly fit unique stories on parchment
Each peeled curiosity a lifetime of exploration
From surface to center
A fascination of humanity
Greatest hope - prayer for open hearts - deep breath
Don't contain, censor, stifle - old spirit - carve river banks - sculpt mountains- run free fierce Tasmanian devil -
You are unusual - gifted
The world is privileged and waiting to see, and a bit frightened
I am interested - but peculiarly always uncomfortable - I am ashamed
Because I fear you - envy you
And feel diminished in your presence

Sparkle

Words, words....shining. Words, words, shining, unique, bright star
Glitter upon glitter - snowflake patterns
This boundless beauty like water colors
Bleeding waterfalls
No moment the same - each second remarkable
Energetic - ecstatic - inspirational passion
Like a woman waiting at a table
Wearing thick fur and pearls
Dazzling, enchanting and burning fast
Cheekbones blushed darkly
Center stage in the circus
Born under a spot light and tethered like a shadow
Some souls can only exist as a main act

Split

Lover - mother
Huntress and gentle touch
Warrior and servant
Humble and fierce
Temptress - maternal
Female dichotomy
How to embody - embrace true nature
How to accept - without shame, guilt, or fear?

Hyacinth

Blue - exquisite blue
Purple tips flirting with sunlight
Morning - like a deep slow breath
Slow exhale and gentle whispers
I listen –

Don't give up

The world churns - layered- kneaded- flour and yeast
Brief glimpses - small windows to shadow self
Ugly - culture defines ugly aspects
And beauty - such beauty - exposed to the sunlight
I have unfaltering faith in you - only you
Buzzing strength through spirit
Solar flair - huntress - Amazon archer
Feel that agitation - harnessed passion - my love, heal
Channel - driven focus - like sharp blinding glare or rhinestone reflection in sunlight
The world squints - but no one looks away

Clearing

Fog is lifting
Love is bleeding in water like dancing fabric
Fading
Reminding me that a dandelion
Once flew from pursed breath
From my lips
Asking to find peace with love
Love believed - eternal
But growth and time would shed it
Giving me faith
This too will come to light - to lift the starry veil
This too will fade - in time - with focus
Dear heart, give it time

Dante

I watched you - so many times
Without direction or persuasion
You are this spirit without guidance
A side walk is busy - you retreat to the grass
Give way for others. Search for lost cats,
Cry if others may suffer even slightly - the potential that you had contribution
Or simply so overwhelmed with emotion
Unable to articulate that feeling
But I am in awe and grateful you let me see a glimpse of it
Run on sentence of out pouring heart
Don't be afraid - you have a gift
My gift - and supported always from my deepest love
You see - we were born unusual - angels
Trying to find ground. Trying to stay in these bodies

Gabriel

Sweetest energy - pure and short burning emotions
Charismatic - open soul
This world was made for you
You entered and owned it
Never doubted your crown
Frustrated when nature didn't support what you knew confidently
Adored
Epic hugs - without fear
Self knowledge - without fear
Only saddened by solitude
And disapproval of love - your way of loving
Bright, bold, fast
Like fire over dry branches
Quick and consuming
But honest - so honest always
I love you like this - raw emotion then gentle embrace - don't ever change

In Love is not a Choice

- 2ⁿᵈ Chapter

Let's be clear - it isn't. Truly isn't
But what I've learned in 6 months is that self love is
And deserves more culturing and nurturing than any other lifetime of loves
Feel what you feel
Be open, be honest, be raw;
Then - simply pay attention
Close attention
How do they respond?
If you ask for something repeatedly, do they ignore it? While you honor their requests.
If you place value on something simple, will they support it? Or say nothing - unless that simple request is theirs.
If you feel one way and they feel another, are their feelings the point of focus and ultimately the decision for your relationship?
What I've learned is being in love in not a choice-
But I can certainly, utterly, completely, and with dignity tell that undeserving 'in love' to either remember what they once worshipped,
Or to step aside - because the line is long
And they can meditate on regret from the end of it

She did rise

That place - ah, that place
Forgotten, misty face
Blurred picture - dignity - pride
The warrior - diminished inside
Dormant, but not truly lost
Slowly layered - pity the cost
Repetitive sacrifice, cowered and shame
Hiding true strength - forgetting her name
Then an ember struck - spark
Brief memory in the dark
Then the spark turned to flame
Burning - no longer tame
Spreading, thawing her skin
Warmed surface moving in
She remembered - again clear
Warriors fight despite fear
And stand - focused, sharp eyes
Her power - once lost - now rise

Printed in the United States
By Bookmasters